Sign Language

A Photograph Album of Visual Puns

Ann Sanfedele

A Citadel Press Book
Published by Carol Publishing Group

A Citadel Press Book
Published by Carol Publishing Group
Citadel Press is a registered trademark of
Carol Communications, Inc.

Editorial Offices   Sales & Distribution Offices
600 Madison Avenue   120 Enterprise Avenue
New York, NY 10022   Secaucus, NJ 07094

In Canada: Canadian Manda Group
P.O. Box 920, Station U
Toronto, Ontario M8Z 5P9

Queries regarding rights and permissions
should be addressed to: Carol Publishing Group,
600 Madison Avenue, New York, NY 10022

Manufactured in the United States of America
10 9 8 7 6 5 4 3 2 1

Carol Publishing Group books are available at special discounts
for bulk purchases, for sales promotions, fund-raising, or
educational purposes. Special editions can also be created to
specifications. For details contact: Special Sales Department,
Carol Publishing Group, 120 Enterprise Ave., Secaucus, NJ 07094

Library of Congress Cataloging-in-Publication Data

Sanfedele, Ann.
    Sign language : a photograph album of visual puns / by Ann Sanfedele.
        p.   cm.
    "A Citadel Press book."
    ISBN 0-8065-1356-X
    1. Photography, Humorous. 2. Signs and signboards — Pictorial works. I. Title.
TR679.5.S27 1992
779' . 092 — dc20   92-20880
                                                                            CIP

For Richard, of course

Acknowledgments

Most importantly, I thank my editor, Gail Kinn, for her savvy eye, insight, and tolerance. To my agent, Anne Edelstein, for all her help in pulling me through my first book contract. And to both Anne and Gail for their enthusiasm for my work.

Thanks to my friends who helped me find some of the subjects I recorded here—especially Sara, Dee, Nora, "Pigdog," and Carol.

And a very special thanks to Jim Piazza, without whose interest this book might not have happened.

—A.S.

Route 44, New Mexico 1990

Vega, Texas 1987

Globe, Arizona 1985

Las Vegas, Nevada 1984

Las Vegas, Nevada 1991

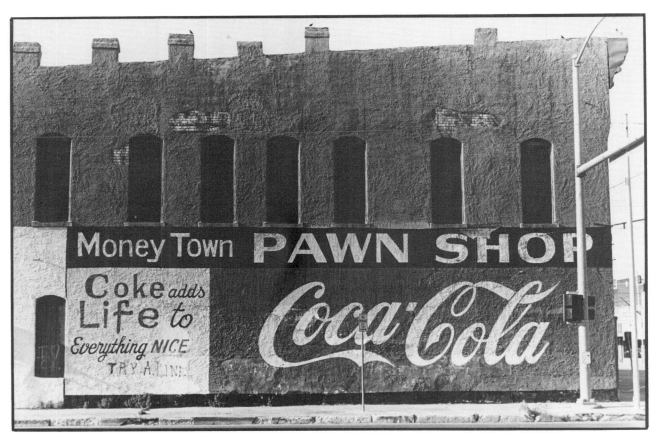

El Reno, Oklahoma 1987

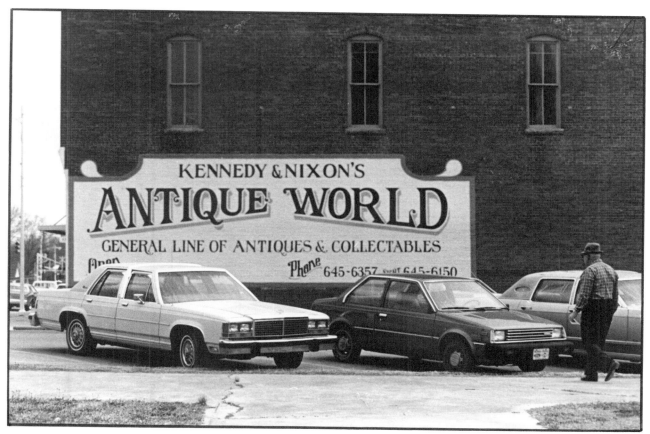

Selmer, Tennessee 1987

Las Vegas, Nevada 1987

Las Vegas, Nevada 1991

Route 70, New Mexico 1985

Port Clyde, Maine 1978

Cortez, Colorado 1990

Route 89, Arizona 1985

Nowhere, Arizona 1982

Goldfield, Nevada 1989

Lordsburg, New Mexico 1985

Newkirk, New Mexico 1987

Route 389, Arizona 1985

Route 58, California 1987

Durant, Oklahoma 1985

Route 94, Montana 1985

Pearce, Arizona 1990

Skagway, Alaska 1989

McAlester, Oklahoma 1985

Morrow, Ohio 1991

Stonington, Connecticut 1985

Vermont 1981

Mountainville, New York 1978

Buffalo, New York 1991

Forrest City, Arizona 1987

Houston, Texas 1985

Peculiar, Montana 1985

Washington, D.C. 1980

Keene, New Hampshire 1979

New York City 1979

Hoboken, New Jersey 1984

New York City 1977

New York City 1979

Monhegan Island, Maine 1978

Monhegan Island, Maine 1978

Providence, Rhode Island 1981

Providence, Rhode Island 1981

Moab, Utah 1986

Cold Spring, New York 1979

New York City 1979

Brimfield, Massachusetts 1977

New York City 1977

New York City 1979

New York City 1978

New York City 1980

Globe, Arizona 1984

Albany, New York 1979

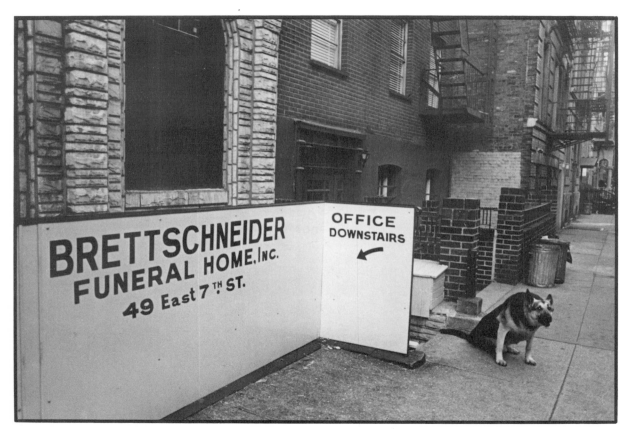

New York City 1979

Pittsfield, Massachusetts 1977

Pittsfield, Massachusetts 1977

Syracuse, New York 1977

Route 94, North Dakota 1989

Deming, New Mexico 1985

White Sands, New Mexico 1985